Greenblatt Business Expense and Mileage Log Book

by

Kim Isaac Greenblatt

Kim Greenblatt Publisher
Published In West Hills, California

Greenblatt Business Expense and Mileage Log Book
by Kim Isaac Greenblatt

Disclosure: You should be aware of the laws and regulations at the Federal and state level where it concerns income taxes. This log book is to be used as a tool to supplement your tax planning throughout the year. Please always remember to be in compliance with Federal and respective State and local tax laws.

Published by Kim Greenblatt,
West Hills, California, United States of America.

ISBN-13   978-1-60622-005-4
April 2010

Dedicated to my clients and anybody who has had to scurry around looking for tax records. Please remember that you should keep great records and remember to start your tax planning at the beginning of each year and not a year later just before the tax season ends.

INTRODUCTION

Hello. My name is Kim Isaac Greenblatt. I am a consultant, run my own publishing company and I prepare income taxes. Even if you already have a great tax person or do your own taxes using one of the various software packages out there the chances are that you may be missing one important aspect of tax law.

You need to substantiate what you are doing especially if you are self-employed. That means that not only do you need to save all your receipts for your work related activities (you are doing that, aren't you?) but you also need to track the details of your business. For those of you who have been audited, you know exactly what I am talking about. For those of you who have never received an Internal Revenue Service or respective state income tax letter, you may want to listen up. We are in a financial Depression and the IRS and states are doing what they can to try to collect more revenue. Guess where they are looking? If you answered, "At me", you are right. This book is to help you in your documentation if you end up getting audited and have to substantiate your business related expenses.

Are you tracking your sales calls? Are you tracking when you make your quarterly Federal estimated income tax payments? More importantly than any of that, are you forecasting and budgeting what kind of money you will need to have to run your business for the upcoming year? It is one thing for tax software packages to ask you about it once a year and another to have a tool that you can use daily to keep you out of trouble.

This book has the traditional business expense logs, mileage logs and as a bonus has a place for you to track your quarterly income tax payments for the Fed and three respective states. The end of the book has an additional set of estimated forms to carry you into a Second Tax Year to get you started.

To use the business budgeting, I have given you 18 months of pages (and one extra budgeting page for good luck) that can be used in any year – you need to just add in the upper right hand corner the month and year that you are tracking information on.

You can always transfer the details over to your respective handheld communication or computer device of choice later on. If you get audited, the IRS will more than likely ask for paper documentation and this book will help (long with your other good recordkeeping and receipts).

I wish you the best and if you need help with your income taxes, drop me a line at kimg@kimgreenblatt.com. I am always looking for new tax clients and I love working with people and income taxes.

Thanks for buying this book. Part of all my proceeds go to finding a cure for Rett Syndrome. Girls are born with the Rett gene once every fifteen minutes. Boys born with the Rett gene generally die at birth. If you are self-employed, this book may qualify as a business related expense. A few other tidbits and then we will get to the log book:

As the economy gets better (and yes, eventually it will one way or another or we all are in trouble), the skills you will develop now will help you as you continue to move up and thrive in the financial food chain.

Happy tax planning and congratulations on taking the steps to better recordkeeping. To quote Benjamin Franklin, “May you be healthy, wealthy and wise”.

Kim Isaac Greenblatt
April 24, 2010
Los Angeles, California

Estimated Fed Tax Payments

Year

Payment Due Dates:	Amount Due:	Date Paid:	Check /money order or credit /debit card confirmation	Total amount paid
4/15				
6/15				
9/15				
1/15 of the next year				

The years have been left out and as of the printing of this book, we are sticking to the 15th for the quarters even though there may be some extended dates (or earlier ones) in some years. For more specific dates please check the IRS at their website: www.irs.gov. Any tax credits that you have as a carry over from previous years are not included in this calculation either.

Estimated State Tax Payments

Year

Payment Due Dates:	Amount Due:	Date Paid:	Check /money order or credit /debit card confirmation	Total amount paid
4/15				
6/15				
9/15				
1/15 of the next year				

The years have been left out and as of the printing of this book, we are sticking to the 15th for the quarters even though there may be some extended dates in some years.

For more specific dates and the appropriate percentages that your state may require you to pay as your estimate, please check your state's specific website.

Estimated State Tax Payments

Year

Payment Due Dates:	Amount Due:	Date Paid:	Check /money order or credit /debit card confirmation	Total amount paid
4/15				
6/15				
9/15				
1/15 of the next year				

The years have been left out and as of the printing of this book, we are sticking to the 15th for the quarters even though there may be some extended dates in some years.

For more specific dates and the appropriate percentages that your state may require you to pay as your estimate, please check your state's specific website.

Estimated State Tax Payments

Year

Payment Due Dates:	Amount Due:	Date Paid:	Check /money order or credit /debit card confirmation	Total amount paid
4/15				
6/15				
9/15				
1/15 of the next year				

The years have been left out and as of the printing of this book, we are sticking to the 15th for the quarters even though there may be some extended dates in some years.

For more specific dates and the appropriate percentages that your state may require you to pay as your estimate, please check your state's specific website.

My Expenses Budgeted

Month / Year

Staffing	Budgeted	Actual	Difference ($)	Difference (%)
Office			$	
Store				
Your Salary or Draw				
Others				
Operating	**Budgeted**	**Actual**	**Difference ($)**	**Difference (%)**
Advertising			$	
Bad debts				
Car and truck expenses				
Cash discounts				
Contractors				
Delivery costs				
Depletion				
Depreciation				
Dues and subscriptions				
Employee benefits				
Insurance				
Interest				
Legal /Professional Svcs				
Maintenance and repairs				
Office Expenses				
Pension & Profit Sharing				
Rent or mortgage				
vehicles machines equip				
other business property				
Repairs & Maintenance				
Shipping and storage				
Supplies				
Taxes/Licenses				
Telephone				
Utilities				
Wages(less emp credits)				
Other				
Total Expenses	**Budgeted**	**Actual**	**Difference ($)**	**Difference (%)**
	$	$	$	

Date:	Start Odometer Reading:	End Odometer Reading:	Miles Travelled:	Purpose (Be Descriptive):	Total Miles:	Meals:	Entertainment:

Date:	Start Odometer Reading:	End Odometer Reading:	Miles Travelled:	Purpose (Be Descriptive):	Total Miles:	Meals:	Entertainment:

MEDICAL INFO TRACKING

Date:	Start Odometer Reading:	End Odometer Reading:	Miles Travelled:	Medical:	Total Miles:	DR/DDS:	Prescriptions:	Hospital/Lab/X-rays:	Supplies:

CHARITABLE CONTRIBUTIONS

Date:	Start Odometer Reading:	End Odometer Reading:	Miles Travelled:	CHARITY NAME:	ADDRESS/TIN:	Amount:	Check/Debit:

My Expenses Budgeted

Month / Year

Staffing	Budgeted	Actual	Difference ($)	Difference (%)
Office			$	
Store				
Your Salary or Draw				
Others				
Operating	**Budgeted**	**Actual**	**Difference ($)**	**Difference (%)**
Advertising			$	
Bad debts				
Car and truck expenses				
Cash discounts				
Contractors				
Delivery costs				
Depletion				
Depreciation				
Dues and subscriptions				
Employee benefits				
Insurance				
Interest				
Legal /Professional Svcs				
Maintenance and repairs				
Office Expenses				
Pension & Profit Sharing				
Rent or mortgage				
vehicles machines equip				
other business property				
Repairs & Maintenance				
Shipping and storage				
Supplies				
Taxes/Licenses				
Telephone				
Utilities				
Wages(less emp credits)				
Other				
Total Expenses	**Budgeted**	**Actual**	**Difference ($)**	**Difference (%)**
	$	$	$	

Date:	Start Odometer Reading:	End Odometer Reading:	Miles Travelled:	Purpose (Be Descriptive):	Total Miles:	Meals:	Entertainment:

Date:	Start Odometer Reading:	End Odometer Reading:	Miles Travelled:	Purpose (Be Descriptive):	Total Miles:	Meals:	Entertainment:

MEDICAL INFO TRACKING

Date:	Start Odometer Reading:	End Odometer Reading:	Miles Travelled:	Medical:	Total Miles:	DR/DDS:	Prescriptions:	Hospital/Lab/X-rays:	Supplies:

CHARITABLE CONTRIBUTIONS

Date:	Start Odometer Reading:	End Odometer Reading:	Miles Travelled:	CHARITY NAME:	ADDRESS/TIN:	Amount:	Check/Debit:

My Expenses Budgeted

Month / Year

Staffing	Budgeted	Actual	Difference ($)	Difference (%)
Office			$	
Store				
Your Salary or Draw				
Others				
Operating	**Budgeted**	**Actual**	**Difference ($)**	**Difference (%)**
Advertising			$	
Bad debts				
Car and truck expenses				
Cash discounts				
Contractors				
Delivery costs				
Depletion				
Depreciation				
Dues and subscriptions				
Employee benefits				
Insurance				
Interest				
Legal /Professional Svcs				
Maintenance and repairs				
Office Expenses				
Pension & Profit Sharing				
Rent or mortgage				
vehicles machines equip				
other business property				
Repairs & Maintenance				
Shipping and storage				
Supplies				
Taxes/Licenses				
Telephone				
Utilities				
Wages(less emp credits)				
Other				
Total Expenses	**Budgeted**	**Actual**	**Difference ($)**	**Difference (%)**
	$	$	$	

Date:	Start Odometer Reading:	End Odometer Reading:	Miles Travelled:	Purpose (Be Descriptive):	Total Miles:	Meals:	Entertainment:

Date:	Start Odometer Reading:	End Odometer Reading:	Miles Travelled:	Purpose (Be Descriptive):	Total Miles:	Meals:	Entertainment:

MEDICAL INFO TRACKING

Date:	Start Odometer Reading:	End Odometer Reading:	Miles Travelled:	Medical:	Total Miles:	DR/DDS:	Prescriptions:	Hospital/Lab/X-rays:	Supplies:

CHARITABLE CONTRIBUTIONS

Date:	Start Odometer Reading:	End Odometer Reading:	Miles Travelled:	CHARITY NAME:	ADDRESS/TIN:	Amount:	Check/Debit:

My Expenses Budgeted

Month / Year

Staffing	Budgeted	Actual	Difference ($)	Difference (%)
Office			$	
Store				
Your Salary or Draw				
Others				
Operating	**Budgeted**	**Actual**	**Difference ($)**	**Difference (%)**
Advertising			$	
Bad debts				
Car and truck expenses				
Cash discounts				
Contractors				
Delivery costs				
Depletion				
Depreciation				
Dues and subscriptions				
Employee benefits				
Insurance				
Interest				
Legal /Professional Svcs				
Maintenance and repairs				
Office Expenses				
Pension & Profit Sharing				
Rent or mortgage				
vehicles machines equip				
other business property				
Repairs & Maintenance				
Shipping and storage				
Supplies				
Taxes/Licenses				
Telephone				
Utilities				
Wages(less emp credits)				
Other				
Total Expenses	**Budgeted**	**Actual**	**Difference ($)**	**Difference (%)**
	$	$	$	

Date:	Start Odometer Reading:	End Odometer Reading:	Miles Travelled:	Purpose (Be Descriptive):	Total Miles:	Meals:	Entertainment:

Date:	Start Odometer Reading:	End Odometer Reading:	Miles Travelled:	Purpose (Be Descriptive):	Total Miles:	Meals:	Entertainment:

MEDICAL INFO TRACKING

Date:	Start Odometer Reading:	End Odometer Reading:	Miles Travelled:	Medical:	Total Miles:	DR/DDS:	Prescriptions:	Hospital/Lab/X-rays:	Supplies:

CHARITABLE CONTRIBUTIONS

Date:	Start Odometer Reading:	End Odometer Reading:	Miles Travelled:	CHARITY NAME:	ADDRESS/TIN:	Amount:	Check/Debit:

My Expenses Budgeted

Month / Year

Staffing	Budgeted	Actual	Difference ($)	Difference (%)
Office			$	
Store				
Your Salary or Draw				
Others				
Operating	**Budgeted**	**Actual**	**Difference ($)**	**Difference (%)**
Advertising			$	
Bad debts				
Car and truck expenses				
Cash discounts				
Contractors				
Delivery costs				
Depletion				
Depreciation				
Dues and subscriptions				
Employee benefits				
Insurance				
Interest				
Legal /Professional Svcs				
Maintenance and repairs				
Office Expenses				
Pension & Profit Sharing				
Rent or mortgage				
vehicles machines equip				
other business property				
Repairs & Maintenance				
Shipping and storage				
Supplies				
Taxes/Licenses				
Telephone				
Utilities				
Wages(less emp credits)				
Other				
Total Expenses	**Budgeted**	**Actual**	**Difference ($)**	**Difference (%)**
	$	$	$	

Date:	Start Odometer Reading:	End Odometer Reading:	Miles Travelled:	Purpose (Be Descriptive):	Total Miles:	Meals:	Entertainment:

Date:	Start Odometer Reading:	End Odometer Reading:	Miles Travelled:	Purpose (Be Descriptive):	Total Miles:	Meals:	Entertainment:

MEDICAL INFO TRACKING

Date:	Start Odometer Reading:	End Odometer Reading:	Miles Travelled:	Medical:	Total Miles:	DR/DDS:	Prescriptions:	Hospital/Lab/X-rays:	Supplies:

CHARITABLE CONTRIBUTIONS

Date:	Start Odometer Reading:	End Odometer Reading:	Miles Travelled:	CHARITY NAME:	ADDRESS/TIN:	Amount:	Check/Debit:

My Expenses Budgeted

Month / Year

Staffing	Budgeted	Actual	Difference ($)	Difference (%)
Office			$	
Store				
Your Salary or Draw				
Others				
Operating	**Budgeted**	**Actual**	**Difference ($)**	**Difference (%)**
Advertising			$	
Bad debts				
Car and truck expenses				
Cash discounts				
Contractors				
Delivery costs				
Depletion				
Depreciation				
Dues and subscriptions				
Employee benefits				
Insurance				
Interest				
Legal /Professional Svcs				
Maintenance and repairs				
Office Expenses				
Pension & Profit Sharing				
Rent or mortgage				
vehicles machines equip				
other business property				
Repairs & Maintenance				
Shipping and storage				
Supplies				
Taxes/Licenses				
Telephone				
Utilities				
Wages(less emp credits)				
Other				
Total Expenses	**Budgeted**	**Actual**	**Difference ($)**	**Difference (%)**
	$	$	$	

Date:	Start Odometer Reading:	End Odometer Reading:	Miles Travelled:	Purpose (Be Descriptive):	Total Miles:	Meals:	Entertainment:

Date:	Start Odometer Reading:	End Odometer Reading:	Miles Travelled:	Purpose (Be Descriptive):	Total Miles:	Meals:	Entertainment:

MEDICAL INFO TRACKING

Date:	Start Odometer Reading:	End Odometer Reading:	Miles Travelled:	Medical:	Total Miles:	DR/DDS:	Prescriptions:	Hospital/Lab/X-rays:	Supplies:

CHARITABLE CONTRIBUTIONS

Date:	Start Odometer Reading:	End Odometer Reading:	Miles Travelled:	CHARITY NAME:	ADDRESS/TIN:	Amount:	Check/Debit:

My Expenses Budgeted

Month / Year

Staffing	Budgeted	Actual	Difference ($)	Difference (%)
Office			$	
Store				
Your Salary or Draw				
Others				
Operating	**Budgeted**	**Actual**	**Difference ($)**	**Difference (%)**
Advertising			$	
Bad debts				
Car and truck expenses				
Cash discounts				
Contractors				
Delivery costs				
Depletion				
Depreciation				
Dues and subscriptions				
Employee benefits				
Insurance				
Interest				
Legal /Professional Svcs				
Maintenance and repairs				
Office Expenses				
Pension & Profit Sharing				
Rent or mortgage				
vehicles machines equip				
other business property				
Repairs & Maintenance				
Shipping and storage				
Supplies				
Taxes/Licenses				
Telephone				
Utilities				
Wages(less emp credits)				
Other				
Total Expenses	**Budgeted**	**Actual**	**Difference ($)**	**Difference (%)**
	$	$	$	

Date:	Start Odometer Reading:	End Odometer Reading:	Miles Travelled:	Purpose (Be Descriptive):	Total Miles:	Meals:	Entertainment:

Date:	Start Odometer Reading:	End Odometer Reading:	Miles Travelled:	Purpose (Be Descriptive):	Total Miles:	Meals:	Entertainment:

MEDICAL INFO TRACKING

Date:	Start Odometer Reading:	End Odometer Reading:	Miles Travelled:	Medical:	Total Miles:	DR/DDS:	Prescriptions:	Hospital/Lab/X-rays:	Supplies:

CHARITABLE CONTRIBUTIONS

Date:	Start Odometer Reading:	End Odometer Reading:	Miles Travelled:	CHARITY NAME:	ADDRESS/TIN:	Amount:	Check/Debit:

My Expenses Budgeted

Month / Year

Staffing	Budgeted	Actual	Difference ($)	Difference (%)
Office			$	
Store				
Your Salary or Draw				
Others				
Operating	**Budgeted**	**Actual**	**Difference ($)**	**Difference (%)**
Advertising			$	
Bad debts				
Car and truck expenses				
Cash discounts				
Contractors				
Delivery costs				
Depletion				
Depreciation				
Dues and subscriptions				
Employee benefits				
Insurance				
Interest				
Legal /Professional Svcs				
Maintenance and repairs				
Office Expenses				
Pension & Profit Sharing				
Rent or mortgage				
vehicles machines equip				
other business property				
Repairs & Maintenance				
Shipping and storage				
Supplies				
Taxes/Licenses				
Telephone				
Utilities				
Wages(less emp credits)				
Other				
Total Expenses	**Budgeted**	**Actual**	**Difference ($)**	**Difference (%)**
	$	$	$	

Date:	Start Odometer Reading:	End Odometer Reading:	Miles Travelled:	Purpose (Be Descriptive):	Total Miles:	Meals:	Entertainment:

Date:	Start Odometer Reading:	End Odometer Reading:	Miles Travelled:	Purpose (Be Descriptive):	Total Miles:	Meals:	Entertainment:

MEDICAL INFO TRACKING

Date:	Start Odometer Reading:	End Odometer Reading:	Miles Travelled:	Medical:	Total Miles:	DR/DDS:	Prescriptions:	Hospital/Lab/X-rays:	Supplies:

CHARITABLE CONTRIBUTIONS

Date:	Start Odometer Reading:	End Odometer Reading:	Miles Travelled:	CHARITY NAME:	ADDRESS/TIN:	Amount:	Check/Debit:

My Expenses Budgeted

Month / Year

Staffing	Budgeted	Actual	Difference ($)	Difference (%)
Office			$	
Store				
Your Salary or Draw				
Others				
Operating	**Budgeted**	**Actual**	**Difference ($)**	**Difference (%)**
Advertising			$	
Bad debts				
Car and truck expenses				
Cash discounts				
Contractors				
Delivery costs				
Depletion				
Depreciation				
Dues and subscriptions				
Employee benefits				
Insurance				
Interest				
Legal /Professional Svcs				
Maintenance and repairs				
Office Expenses				
Pension & Profit Sharing				
Rent or mortgage				
vehicles machines equip				
other business property				
Repairs & Maintenance				
Shipping and storage				
Supplies				
Taxes/Licenses				
Telephone				
Utilities				
Wages(less emp credits)				
Other				
Total Expenses	**Budgeted**	**Actual**	**Difference ($)**	**Difference (%)**
	$	$	$	

Date:	Start Odometer Reading:	End Odometer Reading:	Miles Travelled:	Purpose (Be Descriptive):	Total Miles:	Meals:	Entertainment:

Date:	Start Odometer Reading:	End Odometer Reading:	Miles Travelled:	Purpose (Be Descriptive):	Total Miles:	Meals:	Entertainment:

MEDICAL INFO TRACKING

Date:	Start Odometer Reading:	End Odometer Reading:	Miles Travelled:	Medical:	Total Miles:	DR/DDS:	Prescriptions:	Hospital/Lab/X-rays:	Supplies:

CHARITABLE CONTRIBUTIONS

Date:	Start Odometer Reading:	End Odometer Reading:	Miles Travelled:	CHARITY NAME:	ADDRESS/TIN:	Amount:	Check/Debit:

My Expenses Budgeted

Month / Year

Staffing	Budgeted	Actual	Difference ($)	Difference (%)
Office			$	
Store				
Your Salary or Draw				
Others				
Operating	**Budgeted**	**Actual**	**Difference ($)**	**Difference (%)**
Advertising			$	
Bad debts				
Car and truck expenses				
Cash discounts				
Contractors				
Delivery costs				
Depletion				
Depreciation				
Dues and subscriptions				
Employee benefits				
Insurance				
Interest				
Legal /Professional Svcs				
Maintenance and repairs				
Office Expenses				
Pension & Profit Sharing				
Rent or mortgage				
vehicles machines equip				
other business property				
Repairs & Maintenance				
Shipping and storage				
Supplies				
Taxes/Licenses				
Telephone				
Utilities				
Wages(less emp credits)				
Other				
Total Expenses	**Budgeted**	**Actual**	**Difference ($)**	**Difference (%)**
	$	$	$	

Date:	Start Odometer Reading:	End Odometer Reading:	Miles Travelled:	Purpose (Be Descriptive):	Total Miles:	Meals:	Entertainment:

Date:	Start Odometer Reading:	End Odometer Reading:	Miles Travelled:	Purpose (Be Descriptive):	Total Miles:	Meals:	Entertainment:

MEDICAL INFO TRACKING

Date:	Start Odometer Reading:	End Odometer Reading:	Miles Travelled:	Medical:	Total Miles:	DR/DDS:	Prescriptions:	Hospital/Lab/X-rays:	Supplies:

CHARITABLE CONTRIBUTIONS

Date:	Start Odometer Reading:	End Odometer Reading:	Miles Travelled:	CHARITY NAME:	ADDRESS/TIN:	Amount:	Check/Debit:

My Expenses Budgeted

Month / Year

Staffing	Budgeted	Actual	Difference ($)	Difference (%)
Office			$	
Store				
Your Salary or Draw				
Others				
Operating	**Budgeted**	**Actual**	**Difference ($)**	**Difference (%)**
Advertising			$	
Bad debts				
Car and truck expenses				
Cash discounts				
Contractors				
Delivery costs				
Depletion				
Depreciation				
Dues and subscriptions				
Employee benefits				
Insurance				
Interest				
Legal /Professional Svcs				
Maintenance and repairs				
Office Expenses				
Pension & Profit Sharing				
Rent or mortgage				
vehicles machines equip				
other business property				
Repairs & Maintenance				
Shipping and storage				
Supplies				
Taxes/Licenses				
Telephone				
Utilities				
Wages(less emp credits)				
Other				
Total Expenses	**Budgeted**	**Actual**	**Difference ($)**	**Difference (%)**
	$	$	$	

Date:	Start Odometer Reading:	End Odometer Reading:	Miles Travelled:	Purpose (Be Descriptive):	Total Miles:	Meals:	Entertainment:

Date:	Start Odometer Reading:	End Odometer Reading:	Miles Travelled:	Purpose (Be Descriptive):	Total Miles:	Meals:	Entertainment:

MEDICAL INFO TRACKING

Date:	Start Odometer Reading:	End Odometer Reading:	Miles Travelled:	Medical:	Total Miles:	DR/DDS:	Prescriptions:	Hospital/Lab/X-rays:	Supplies:

CHARITABLE CONTRIBUTIONS

Date:	Start Odometer Reading:	End Odometer Reading:	Miles Travelled:	CHARITY NAME:	ADDRESS/TIN:	Amount:	Check/Debit:

My Expenses Budgeted

Month / Year

Staffing	Budgeted	Actual	Difference ($)	Difference (%)
Office			$	
Store				
Your Salary or Draw				
Others				
Operating	**Budgeted**	**Actual**	**Difference ($)**	**Difference (%)**
Advertising			$	
Bad debts				
Car and truck expenses				
Cash discounts				
Contractors				
Delivery costs				
Depletion				
Depreciation				
Dues and subscriptions				
Employee benefits				
Insurance				
Interest				
Legal /Professional Svcs				
Maintenance and repairs				
Office Expenses				
Pension & Profit Sharing				
Rent or mortgage				
vehicles machines equip				
other business property				
Repairs & Maintenance				
Shipping and storage				
Supplies				
Taxes/Licenses				
Telephone				
Utilities				
Wages(less emp credits)				
Other				
Total Expenses	**Budgeted**	**Actual**	**Difference ($)**	**Difference (%)**
	$	$	$	

Date:	Start Odometer Reading:	End Odometer Reading:	Miles Travelled:	Purpose (Be Descriptive):	Total Miles:	Meals:	Entertainment:

Date:	Start Odometer Reading:	End Odometer Reading:	Miles Travelled:	Purpose (Be Descriptive):	Total Miles:	Meals:	Entertainment:

MEDICAL INFO TRACKING

Date:	Start Odometer Reading:	End Odometer Reading:	Miles Travelled:	Medical:	Total Miles:	DR/DDS:	Prescriptions:	Hospital/Lab/X-rays:	Supplies:

CHARITABLE CONTRIBUTIONS

Date:	Start Odometer Reading:	End Odometer Reading:	Miles Travelled:	CHARITY NAME:	ADDRESS/TIN:	Amount:	Check/Debit:

My Expenses Budgeted

Month / Year

Staffing	Budgeted	Actual	Difference ($)	Difference (%)
Office			$	
Store				
Your Salary or Draw				
Others				
Operating	**Budgeted**	**Actual**	**Difference ($)**	**Difference (%)**
Advertising			$	
Bad debts				
Car and truck expenses				
Cash discounts				
Contractors				
Delivery costs				
Depletion				
Depreciation				
Dues and subscriptions				
Employee benefits				
Insurance				
Interest				
Legal /Professional Svcs				
Maintenance and repairs				
Office Expenses				
Pension & Profit Sharing				
Rent or mortgage				
vehicles machines equip				
other business property				
Repairs & Maintenance				
Shipping and storage				
Supplies				
Taxes/Licenses				
Telephone				
Utilities				
Wages(less emp credits)				
Other				
Total Expenses	**Budgeted**	**Actual**	**Difference ($)**	**Difference (%)**
	$	$	$	

Date:	Start Odometer Reading:	End Odometer Reading:	Miles Travelled:	Purpose (Be Descriptive):	Total Miles:	Meals:	Entertainment:

Date:	Start Odometer Reading:	End Odometer Reading:	Miles Travelled:	Purpose (Be Descriptive):	Total Miles:	Meals:	Entertainment:

MEDICAL INFO TRACKING

Date:	Start Odometer Reading:	End Odometer Reading:	Miles Travelled:	Medical:	Total Miles:	DR/DDS:	Prescriptions:	Hospital/Lab/X-rays:	Supplies:

CHARITABLE CONTRIBUTIONS

Date:	Start Odometer Reading:	End Odometer Reading:	Miles Travelled:	CHARITY NAME:	ADDRESS/TIN:	Amount:	Check/Debit:

My Expenses Budgeted

Month / Year

Staffing	Budgeted	Actual	Difference ($)	Difference (%)
Office			$	
Store				
Your Salary or Draw				
Others				
Operating	**Budgeted**	**Actual**	**Difference ($)**	**Difference (%)**
Advertising			$	
Bad debts				
Car and truck expenses				
Cash discounts				
Contractors				
Delivery costs				
Depletion				
Depreciation				
Dues and subscriptions				
Employee benefits				
Insurance				
Interest				
Legal /Professional Svcs				
Maintenance and repairs				
Office Expenses				
Pension & Profit Sharing				
Rent or mortgage				
vehicles machines equip				
other business property				
Repairs & Maintenance				
Shipping and storage				
Supplies				
Taxes/Licenses				
Telephone				
Utilities				
Wages(less emp credits)				
Other				
Total Expenses	**Budgeted**	**Actual**	**Difference ($)**	**Difference (%)**
	$	$	$	

Date:	Start Odometer Reading:	End Odometer Reading:	Miles Travelled:	Purpose (Be Descriptive):	Total Miles:	Meals:	Entertainment:

Date:	Start Odometer Reading:	End Odometer Reading:	Miles Travelled:	Purpose (Be Descriptive):	Total Miles:	Meals:	Entertainment:

MEDICAL INFO TRACKING

Date:	Start Odometer Reading:	End Odometer Reading:	Miles Travelled:	Medical:	Total Miles:	DR/DDS:	Prescriptions:	Hospital/Lab/X-rays:	Supplies:

CHARITABLE CONTRIBUTIONS

Date:	Start Odometer Reading:	End Odometer Reading:	Miles Travelled:	CHARITY NAME:	ADDRESS/TIN:	Amount:	Check/Debit:

My Expenses Budgeted

Month / Year

Staffing	Budgeted	Actual	Difference ($)	Difference (%)
Office			$	
Store				
Your Salary or Draw				
Others				
Operating	**Budgeted**	**Actual**	**Difference ($)**	**Difference (%)**
Advertising			$	
Bad debts				
Car and truck expenses				
Cash discounts				
Contractors				
Delivery costs				
Depletion				
Depreciation				
Dues and subscriptions				
Employee benefits				
Insurance				
Interest				
Legal /Professional Svcs				
Maintenance and repairs				
Office Expenses				
Pension & Profit Sharing				
Rent or mortgage				
vehicles machines equip				
other business property				
Repairs & Maintenance				
Shipping and storage				
Supplies				
Taxes/Licenses				
Telephone				
Utilities				
Wages(less emp credits)				
Other				
Total Expenses	**Budgeted**	**Actual**	**Difference ($)**	**Difference (%)**
	$	$	$	

Date:	Start Odometer Reading:	End Odometer Reading:	Miles Travelled:	Purpose (Be Descriptive):	Total Miles:	Meals:	Entertainment:

Date:	Start Odometer Reading:	End Odometer Reading:	Miles Travelled:	Purpose (Be Descriptive):	Total Miles:	Meals:	Entertainment:

MEDICAL INFO TRACKING

Date:	Start Odometer Reading:	End Odometer Reading:	Miles Travelled:	Medical:	Total Miles:	DR/DDS:	Prescriptions:	Hospital/Lab/X-rays:	Supplies:

CHARITABLE CONTRIBUTIONS

Date:	Start Odometer Reading:	End Odometer Reading:	Miles Travelled:	CHARITY NAME:	ADDRESS/TIN:	Amount:	Check/Debit:

My Expenses Budgeted

Month / Year

Staffing	Budgeted	Actual	Difference ($)	Difference (%)
Office			$	
Store				
Your Salary or Draw				
Others				
Operating	**Budgeted**	**Actual**	**Difference ($)**	**Difference (%)**
Advertising			$	
Bad debts				
Car and truck expenses				
Cash discounts				
Contractors				
Delivery costs				
Depletion				
Depreciation				
Dues and subscriptions				
Employee benefits				
Insurance				
Interest				
Legal /Professional Svcs				
Maintenance and repairs				
Office Expenses				
Pension & Profit Sharing				
Rent or mortgage				
vehicles machines equip				
other business property				
Repairs & Maintenance				
Shipping and storage				
Supplies				
Taxes/Licenses				
Telephone				
Utilities				
Wages(less emp credits)				
Other				
Total Expenses	**Budgeted**	**Actual**	**Difference ($)**	**Difference (%)**
	$	$	$	

Date:	Start Odometer Reading:	End Odometer Reading:	Miles Travelled:	Purpose (Be Descriptive):	Total Miles:	Meals:	Entertainment:

Date:	Start Odometer Reading:	End Odometer Reading:	Miles Travelled:	Purpose (Be Descriptive):	Total Miles:	Meals:	Entertainment:

MEDICAL INFO TRACKING

Date:	Start Odometer Reading:	End Odometer Reading:	Miles Travelled:	Medical:	Total Miles:	DR/DDS:	Prescriptions:	Hospital/Lab/X-rays:	Supplies:

CHARITABLE CONTRIBUTIONS

Date:	Start Odometer Reading:	End Odometer Reading:	Miles Travelled:	CHARITY NAME:	ADDRESS/TIN:	Amount:	Check/Debit:

My Expenses Budgeted

Month / Year

Staffing	Budgeted	Actual	Difference ($)	Difference (%)
Office			$	
Store				
Your Salary or Draw				
Others				
Operating	**Budgeted**	**Actual**	**Difference ($)**	**Difference (%)**
Advertising			$	
Bad debts				
Car and truck expenses				
Cash discounts				
Contractors				
Delivery costs				
Depletion				
Depreciation				
Dues and subscriptions				
Employee benefits				
Insurance				
Interest				
Legal /Professional Svcs				
Maintenance and repairs				
Office Expenses				
Pension & Profit Sharing				
Rent or mortgage				
vehicles machines equip				
other business property				
Repairs & Maintenance				
Shipping and storage				
Supplies				
Taxes/Licenses				
Telephone				
Utilities				
Wages(less emp credits)				
Other				
Total Expenses	**Budgeted**	**Actual**	**Difference ($)**	**Difference (%)**
	$	$	$	

Date:	Start Odometer Reading:	End Odometer Reading:	Miles Travelled:	Purpose (Be Descriptive):	Total Miles:	Meals:	Entertainment:

Date:	Start Odometer Reading:	End Odometer Reading:	Miles Travelled:	Purpose (Be Descriptive):	Total Miles:	Meals:	Entertainment:

MEDICAL INFO TRACKING

Date:	Start Odometer Reading:	End Odometer Reading:	Miles Travelled:	Medical:	Total Miles:	DR/DDS:	Prescriptions:	Hospital/Lab/X-rays:	Supplies:

CHARITABLE CONTRIBUTIONS

Date:	Start Odometer Reading:	End Odometer Reading:	Miles Travelled:	CHARITY NAME:	ADDRESS/TIN:	Amount:	Check/Debit:

My Expenses Budgeted

Month / Year

Staffing	Budgeted	Actual	Difference ($)	Difference (%)
Office			$	
Store				
Your Salary or Draw				
Others				
Operating	**Budgeted**	**Actual**	**Difference ($)**	**Difference (%)**
Advertising			$	
Bad debts				
Car and truck expenses				
Cash discounts				
Contractors				
Delivery costs				
Depletion				
Depreciation				
Dues and subscriptions				
Employee benefits				
Insurance				
Interest				
Legal /Professional Svcs				
Maintenance and repairs				
Office Expenses				
Pension & Profit Sharing				
Rent or mortgage				
vehicles machines equip				
other business property				
Repairs & Maintenance				
Shipping and storage				
Supplies				
Taxes/Licenses				
Telephone				
Utilities				
Wages(less emp credits)				
Other				
Total Expenses	**Budgeted**	**Actual**	**Difference ($)**	**Difference (%)**
	$	$	$	

Date:	Start Odometer Reading:	End Odometer Reading:	Miles Travelled:	Purpose (Be Descriptive):	Total Miles:	Meals:	Entertainment:

Date:	Start Odometer Reading:	End Odometer Reading:	Miles Travelled:	Purpose (Be Descriptive):	Total Miles:	Meals:	Entertainment:

MEDICAL INFO TRACKING

Date:	Start Odometer Reading:	End Odometer Reading:	Miles Travelled:	Medical:	Total Miles:	DR/DDS:	Prescriptions:	Hospital/Lab/X-rays:	Supplies:

CHARITABLE CONTRIBUTIONS

Date:	Start Odometer Reading:	End Odometer Reading:	Miles Travelled:	CHARITY NAME:	ADDRESS/TIN:	Amount:	Check/Debit:

My Expenses Budgeted

Month / Year

Staffing	Budgeted	Actual	Difference ($)	Difference (%)
Office			$	
Store				
Your Salary or Draw				
Others				
Operating	**Budgeted**	**Actual**	**Difference ($)**	**Difference (%)**
Advertising			$	
Bad debts				
Car and truck expenses				
Cash discounts				
Contractors				
Delivery costs				
Depletion				
Depreciation				
Dues and subscriptions				
Employee benefits				
Insurance				
Interest				
Legal /Professional Svcs				
Maintenance and repairs				
Office Expenses				
Pension & Profit Sharing				
Rent or mortgage				
vehicles machines equip				
other business property				
Repairs & Maintenance				
Shipping and storage				
Supplies				
Taxes/Licenses				
Telephone				
Utilities				
Wages(less emp credits)				
Other				
Total Expenses	**Budgeted**	**Actual**	**Difference ($)**	**Difference (%)**
	$	$	$	

Date:	Start Odometer Reading:	End Odometer Reading:	Miles Travelled:	Purpose (Be Descriptive):	Total Miles:	Meals:	Entertainment:

Date:	Start Odometer Reading:	End Odometer Reading:	Miles Travelled:	Purpose (Be Descriptive):	Total Miles:	Meals:	Entertainment:

MEDICAL INFO TRACKING

Date:	Start Odometer Reading:	End Odometer Reading:	Miles Travelled:	Medical:	Total Miles:	DR/DDS:	Prescriptions:	Hospital/Lab/X-rays:	Supplies:

CHARITABLE CONTRIBUTIONS

Date:	Start Odometer Reading:	End Odometer Reading:	Miles Travelled:	CHARITY NAME:	ADDRESS/TIN:	Amount:	Check/Debit:

Tax Preparation Checklist: Things to Bring When Visiting a Tax Professional

Personal Data

❒ Social Security Numbers (including spouse and children)

❒ Child care provider tax I.D. or Social Security Number

Employment & Income Data

❒ W-2 forms for this year

❒ Tax refunds and unemployment compensation: Form 1099-G

❒ Miscellaneous income including rent: Form 1099-MISC

❒ Partnership and trust income

❒ Pensions and annuities

❒ Alimony received

❒ Jury duty pay

❒ Gambling and lottery winnings

❒ Prizes and awards

❒ Scholarships and fellowships

❒ State and local income tax refunds

❒ Unemployment compensation

Homeowner/Renter Data

❒ Residential address(es) for this year

❒ Mortgage interest: Form 1098

❒ Sale of your home or other real estate: Form 1099-S

❒ Second mortgage interest paid

❒ Real estate taxes paid

❒ Rent paid during tax year

❒ Moving expenses

Financial Assets

❒ Interest income statements: Form 1099-INT & 1099-OID

❒ Dividend income statements: Form 1099-DIV

❒ Proceeds from broker transactions: Form 1099-B **and the basis of the transactions**

❒ Retirement plan distribution: Form 1099-R

❒ Capital gains or losses

Financial Liabilities

❒ Auto loans and leases (account numbers and car value) **if vehicle used for business**

❒ Student loan interest paid

❒ Early withdrawal penalties on CDs and other time deposits

Automobiles

❒ Personal property tax information

❒ Department of Motor Vehicles fees

Expenses

❒ Gifts to charity (receipts for any single donations of $250 or more and letters from organizations)

❒ Unreimbursed mileage related to volunteer work

❒ Unreimbursed expenses related to your job (travel expenses, entertainment, uniforms,union dues, subscriptions)

❒ Investment expenses

❒ Job-hunting expenses

❒ Education expenses (tuition and fees)

❒ Child care expenses

❒ Medical Savings Accounts

- ❒ Adoption expenses
- ❒ Alimony paid
- ❒ Tax return preparation expenses and fees

Self-Employment Data

- ❒ Estimated tax vouchers for the current year
- ❒ Self-employment tax
- ❒ Self-employment SEP plans
- ❒ Self-employed health insurance
- ❒ K-1s on all partnerships
- ❒ Receipts or documentation for business-related expenses
- ❒ Farm income

Deduction Documents

- ❒ State and local income taxes
- ❒ IRA, Keogh and other retirement plan contributions
- ❒ Medical expenses
- ❒ Casualty or theft losses
- ❒ Other miscellaneous deductions

Other Items

Notes:

Estimated Fed Tax Payments

Year

Payment Due Dates:	Amount Due:	Date Paid:	Check /money order or credit /debit card confirmation	Total amount paid
4/15				
6/15				
9/15				
1/15 of the next year				

The years have been left out and as of the printing of this book, we are sticking to the 15th for the quarters even though there may be some extended dates (or earlier ones) in some years. For more specific dates please check the IRS at their website: www.irs.gov. Any tax credits that you have as a carry over from previous years are not included in this calculation either.

Estimated State Tax Payments

Year

Payment Due Dates:	Amount Due:	Date Paid:	Check /money order or credit /debit card confirmation	Total amount paid
4/15				
6/15				
9/15				
1/15 of the next year				

The years have been left out and as of the printing of this book, we are sticking to the 15th for the quarters even though there may be some extended dates in some years.

For more specific dates and the appropriate percentages that your state may require you to pay as your estimate, please check your state's specific website.

www.ingramcontent.com/pod-product-compliance
Lightning Source LLC
LaVergne TN
LVHW081319060426
835509LV00015B/1596
* 9 7 8 1 6 0 6 2 2 0 0 5 4 *